Nostos

Volume II, Number 1
2018

Lawrence Tjernell, Editor

ISBN-10:
0-692-95360-4

ISBN-13:
978-0-692-95360-0

Longship Press

Printed in the United States

Longship Press 1122 4th Street San Rafael, California 94901

For Jack

Acknowledgments and Appreciations

Some of the poems in this edition of *Nostos* are reprinted. I would like to acknowledge gratefully the following publications and authors.

Andy Plumb/Selena Anne: "be her now" and "she painted me away," *Doll Hearts*, Blue Rain Press, Larkspur, 2016.

Emily Wolahan and Owen Brown: *The Fieldwork Scroll*, eight original scrolls, Magnolia Editions.

Roy Mash: "Two Saints of Clarity," *River Styx*, Vol. 87, 2012. "Hardly Lord Jim," *The Sow's Ear*, Winter, 2012. "Revolving Sunglass Display," *The West Marin Review*, Vol 7, 2016.

I want to thank especially Rebecca Foust, Lisa Rappoport, and David Rollison for having alerted fine writers and artists about the call for submissions for this edition.

Cover Art: Detail from the *Fieldwork Scroll*, by Emily Wolahan and Owen Brown. See pages 63 and 69.

Table of Contents

Elegy, In Extremity

Imagine for a moment a Viet Nam-era Marine Corps sergeant, a veteran of jungle firefights, a Corps wrestler, a square-jawed jarhead, a wide-set leatherneck. Now imagine him emerging from that camouflaged chrysalis into a realm of fatherhood, art, and individuation, through a Metamorphosis, by both Ovid and Kafka — a student of change, its impediments, and its imperatives. This is Jack. He was my friend. No man could ask for a better.

As death approached, Jack said that he had won. Neither of us wanted to be the last man, certainly not without the other to grouse with, fish with, drink with, or play chess with even after we had forgotten either the place we held in the game or the purpose of the pieces themselves. So I lost that contest. Death's sting is felt by the one left living, left with the requirements of elegy.

In his *New Yorker* (September 2017) essay "The Poetry of Death," Donald Hall points out that "poetry begins with elegy, in extremity, as Gilgamesh laments the death of his companion Enkidu ….

Homer sings of heroes as they die in battle, and Priam weeps to see the body of his son Hector dragged around the walls of Troy." I am reminded of the story of King David in 2 Samuel, when after hearing of the death of his son, David weeps, "O my son Absalom, my son, my son Absalom! Would God I had died for thee, O Absalom, my son, my son!" The cry of grief itself an elegy.

This edition of Nostos presents the work of twelve poets, two short-fiction writers, and an artist collaborating with a poet. Through much of their work we hear and see the presence of Death, the long distant wail of loss, the sharp edge of apprehension and fear, the low moan of need. To be sure, not all the works of this edition are elegiac. No theme was called for. But many of these writers' and artist's works orbit around a center, a kind of mournful gravity.

Let this in its sum be an elegiac verse, one that sings a mournful song of loss, beautiful in its course and swell. What better way than through poetry and story and art? This elegy may make the stomach fall and grip; it may salt the eye, make bitter the tongue. But these pages harken to the ancient in form and plea; they shout not just dismay but also praise. Through these pages I hear the song, and its beauty and its sorrow help make a part of my elegy, an elegy for Jack. What better way?

Joe Lamb

Joe Lamb's poetry and essays have appeared in *Earth Island Journal*, *The Sun*, *Caliban*, *Wind*, *Orion*, and other magazines. His work is also included in the anthologies *The Rag and Bone Shop of the Heart: A Poetry Anthology*, Robert Bly *et al.*, editors, and *Veterans of War/Veterans of Peace*, Maxine Hong Kingston editor. Joe founded the Borneo Project, to help the indigenous peoples of Borneo secure land rights and protect their forest. Honored by the Goldman Foundation as an "environmental hero," Joe was featured in the San Francisco public television program, "Green Means." He lives in Berkeley, California.

Conversation With Paul, Bearer of the Story Without an End

Enough about me already,
let's talk about you.

Sure, I'm confused, a little angry, unhinged,
blown open really, and sad, deeply sad,

But that's chump change,
a mosquito in the cathedral.

What matters now,
what really matters.

is that you don't answer,
that you're as silent as

Bergman's God.
And here I am adrift

on the iceberg
of memory,

crying and shivering,
repressing unwanted outbreaks

of unseemly laughter,
talking to whoever it is that listens

when I'm talking
to myself.

Now that you have
all the time in the world

can you find the time
to tell me why?

I never found the time
to confide that your skin

reminded me of well tanned leather,
soft, yet protective,

strong, and, above all,
utilitarian.

Or that your stories
seemed to me like pieces

of an intricate and
surrealistic clock,

bigger than Big Ben,
big enough to fill Dali's warehouse,

a magical profusion of cogs and wheels,
of springs and gizmos,

not inert metal —
a living place

where people move
inside the machine

like Charlie Chaplin,
in *Modern Times*,

sliding through the gears,
oil can in hand,

a perfectly natural
union of man and metal and time.

Your time piece
remained always under construction,

like Gaudi's Sagrada Familia,
alluringly enigmatic, never finished.

Does time have meaning
where you are now?

Does now have any meaning
where you are now?

If it will loosen your tongue
I'll make you a deal;

For my part, I'll read every scrap
you've left behind

If you'll agree to answer just one
of the following three questions:

When you killed yourself,
and your family found you

hanging like some still born chrysalis
of a giant moth,

did you really intend to end your life,
or was this a tragic attempt to molt,

to shed some calcified memory
chaffing unbearably, always out of reach?

If that is too personal,
then unravel for me please

why you chose to take your life
in the writer's cottage you built,

in the room of your own,
in the place where you could

connect the crown wheel to the winding clutch,
adjust the hairspring,

and set the hands of your writerly clock
to whatever time you chose?

If unable, or unwilling,
to answer either of the above,

at least give me a hint why,
the last time I saw you alive,

you brought a length of rope
to our veteran writers' group

and showed me how
to make an intricate knot

that, for the life of me,
I cannot remember how to untie.

Thirteen Ways a Blackbird is Looking at You

1.

On a street below
amid twenty moving feet
the blackbird eyes
a crust of pizza.

2.

Uncertain whether to fly North,
or South, or not at all
the blackbird watches the shadows
of three people approach her tree.

3.

Amid the swirling flock
of a thousand blackbirds
the man with binoculars
became a small part
of the pantomime.

4.

"A man and a woman
Are one.
A man and a woman and a blackbird
Are one."

5.
Images of blackbirds
printed on her blouse
drew one look,
but not a second.

6.
Shotguns filled the pickup's window.
The blackbird flew behind the men
driving to and fro.

7.
O' fat men of Wall Street
why do you worship the Golden Calf?
Look how the black birds
hunt for earthworms
in your cemetery.

8.
Looking up
the blackbird confused
the landing airplane's roar
for the Apocalypse.

9.
Startled by the rag flapping
atop a skinny, branchless tree
the blackbird found refuge
in a metal dumpster
warm with rotting apples.

10.
At the sight of the freeway
undulating with red light
the blackbird cried out sharply.

11.
Picking at the fishing line
tangled around his foot
fear pierced the blackbird.

12.
Perched on the armor
of the fallen samurai
the blackbird cocked his head
and looked into his eye.

13.
It was afternoon all day.
It wasn't snowing;
it hadn't snowed;
and it wasn't going to snow.
The blackbird sat
on the phone line
and listened
with her feet.

Stanza four is from "Thirteen Ways of Looking at a Blackbird," by Wallace Stevens.

Hazel, Yes Hazel

What was the sun thinking when he talked this tree
into making a durian,
the spiky queen of stinky fruits?

We no longer remember the time when thought, tree, and sun
were words that fit together as neatly as
dendrites, photosynthesis,
and nuclear fusion.

Linnaeus said that without knowledge of its name,
memory of the thing itself
vanishes.

But names have small fingers
that hold only
what we let them.

I hold onto the name
of the first girl I ever kissed,
but can no longer remember

the color of her eyes.
We were ten.
Later that year I learned

why her father was never home.
Fifty years later
I can almost feel

her shoulders trembling,
can almost feel the sidewalk
beneath us vanishing.

The Buddhist Marten

If you could accept a small token
from everyone who has hurt you —
perhaps an arrowhead, a blue jay feather,
a pebble resembling a face —

and re-gift them as offerings
to everyone whom you have hurt

you might then understand
that when pursuing
the snowshoe hare
across the frozen lake
it is empathy guiding
the predator
to its prey.

Knowing what the rabbit feels
allows the marten to anticipate,
and thereby mimic,
each movement
of the fleeing hare

edging slightly closer
with each attempt
at evasion
until the
gap closes
and two
become
one.

David Rollison

David Rollison moved to San Francisco in the late summer of 1963 where he studied with Kay Boyle, John Gardner, Leonard Wolf, Jack Gilbert, and others. After 42 years of teaching poetry, first in Santa Maria, California, and then Marin County, he retired, living on the edge of San Pablo Bay where it intersects the Petaluma River. He and his wife walk the bayland wetlands every morning, in the morning mist. Sometimes, in the afternoon, he can write a poem. His recent collection is *Ghost Poems & Wetland Ballads*.

Bamboo Chimes

Keen to the nuance, my friend
smiles at the clacking
of bamboo chimes.
It's a small breeze they need
to strike the lacquered, carved bones
of bamboo into a clamor;
and it's a trained ear you need
for all the voices of the wind.

Folksinger

"I'll call for pen and ink and write my mind."

There was young Shakespeare who would
not clerk in the civic world, who studied
the un-measurable.
On the cobblestone,
wet with a summer shower, he watched
the boy and girl
who had ducked in the alley,
out of the rain, only to find themselves
alone and sheltered.
He sees their eyes and their restless hands,
he breathes in when they breathe in,
and he thinks of marble statures,
and harpsichords,
and the cold sea.
The alley's his world.
The fleeting monuments of the alley
are all he needs to see.
He'll know every part
before they even start
the show.

Brass Handles

When Bruce Conner got old and sick,
      it got harder to get around, and so
                              he put brass handles
                                    all over his house
                  up and down the stairs,
                        in the kitchen,
            in the bathroom,
        everywhere, and,
hand over hand,
holding tight,
            and sometimes, for long,
to the handles,
he could move about,
as he wanted.   He kept his eye keen,
            as he placed them, eyeing
   their size and shape and placement,
so they gleam,
   like an old poem,
     written in old age,
        out on a precipice,
          over the pines,
            over the rushing water,
              set in the waning world,
at last.

Ambition

Ambition's not really found at the top
of a leap, or
in a jeweled and marbled sanctum
or in a laurel chair.
Or if to get there takes ambition.
then it's cheap ambition, sold too soon.
Ambition that costs a pound of flesh
was never filmed in a glittering studio,
high above the avenues, when the dancer's leap,
high and beautiful soared across the transom windows
or part of being out on the highway to Oregon,
climbing the Sierras, watching Shasta rise up stark,
disappear, and then rise up again, the singer finding
the note and word that echo in the heart,
or when sitting by the arched window in the waning light,
the hint of rain fragrant in the air, the poet
forsakes success.   Ambition, stern
ambition is the young diver
up on the granite cliff
above the glimmering water
soaring down like Icarus
and no one
watching.

Joanne Esser

Joanne Esser writes poetry and nonfiction in Minneapolis, Minnesota. She has also been a teacher of young children for over thirty years. She earned an MFA in Creative Writing from Hamline University and published a chapbook of poems, *I Have Always Wanted Lightening*, with Finishing Line Press in 2012. Her work appears in many literary journals, including *Common Ground Review*, *The Sow's Ear Poetry Review*, *Welter*, *Gyroscope Review*, *Temenos*, *and Water-Stone Review*.

Mine

There is so little that is truly mine.
Not my bones, my muscles or blood,
Which I am only borrowing

From the matter that once scattered
Through the universe at the moment
Of the Big Bang, and which,

Assembled into the strong configuration
I am lucky to inhabit
Is serving me well all these years.

Perhaps only the view behind my eyeballs,
My particular perspective,
The accumulated memories I carry

In the purse of my mind
Wrapped like old hard candies
In Kleenex, to be taken out,

A bit dusty and worse for the wear,
And savored when I long to recall.
My name is also mine,

Though unknown others might have used it
Before me. And my heart, worn over time
But still beating, overly soft and easy

To bruise, has become utterly my own.
Though given to me unearned at birth,
It has been shaped, molded, eroded

By stories only I can tell
And tears that are mine alone
Until it has acquired its unique shape.

Yet even this I will have to give back
At the end, grateful for the way
It has held up long enough

To accumulate all that it carries.

My Father's Closet

The boxes wait, big and empty,
for the clothes he won't be wearing any more.
The once-familiar creak of the sliding closet door
sounds too loud in the silent house.

When I was little, I'd sneak in here,
rummage behind the shoe racks,
his neckties hanging down
like vines in a dark woods.
I'd part them to glimpse hidden
Christmas presents. Sometimes I'd try on
his too-big shoes, stomp around him
as he tied his tie in front of the dresser mirror.
Or I'd sift through pieces of gift-wrap paper
and bows of every color,
arrange them in a rainbow on the big bed.
Today I've already pulled out everything from the back,
sorted it dispassionately, thrown stuff away,
the efficient, organized oldest daughter.

Now here are his suits,
lined up, stiff-shouldered, neatly pressed.
I'd never noticed how much gray he wore,
the sameness of the tweeds, steadfast and predictable.
I flip through the hangers, sliding three-piece suits,
his lawyer's uniforms, along the rack.
Evidence of my father slips out in bits:

wisps of old cigar smoke smell,
then a sudden spicy cologne scent I have always known.
A row of shirts, white and white and pale blue and white,
even one with a ballpoint pen still stuck in the pocket,
cling stubbornly to their hangers.
They begin to whisper to me, these shirts,
these navy and burgundy and gray-striped ties,
these suits – his unsentimental, unshakeable voice.
I hear the murmur of years, harsh
and tender, a confused cacophony.

I move slowly now, watching my own hands
as if they might be someone else's.
The feel of a gray padded shoulder
surprises my fingers with its warmth.
I lean into the closet.
When did I get tall enough
to put my face into his shoulder?
I rub my face on a limp sleeve,
close my eyes; the rough fabric
like the maleness of his unshaven face,
giving me a "beard rub" when I was six.
I lift the wide shoulders; the jacket slips off
into my arms, at last released.
I wrap myself around the lifeless form.
It crushes easily under my touch.
We sink into the closet's thick, gray shadows.

Twenty Questions

(After Jim Moore)

How can I describe snow that drifts down this whitely in the morning? What words could possibly hold that lightness? How long will I allow myself to stand here by this window? Why does it remind me of a day when I was a child? Were my mittens red, the ones my grandmother knit for me from wool? Did I know then how those mittens would follow me all these years? When did I lose them? Where are they now? Who else remembers radiators like we used to have, where we laid soggy mittens to dry? Is that why I chose this house, for those same radiators under the windows? Do I deserve such joy as this? What have I done that makes me worthy? Or is it only luck? If so, will it change one day, my winter-piled happiness, into its empty twin? Why worry about that when the sky is so fluffy? Will I spend all day looking? Would that be enough? Or will I follow the soft sounds out the door? Will I find the fullness of my desire as flakes float into white waves that muffle my own footsteps? Or will I just let myself wander in the pleasant mystery of so many unanswered questions?

Heather Ringo

Heather Ringo is a "genre-promiscuous, over-hyphenating writer-activist." Her academic writing has won the E.L. Bartlett Prize in Literary Criticism, and her creative writing has been published in *Educe*, *Psychological Poems: A Journal of Outsider Poetry*, and *The Smoking Poet*. She has also written for *The Tobacco Valley News* and *Drink Me Magazine*. If there is an overarching theme to her work, it is inspiring her readers to find beauty in the ugliest places.

During the Drought

composed on November 9th, 2016

The desert gaped,
a grey dust ocean
teeming with,
all things considered,
strangely resilient creatures:

crepuscular,
they creep out
when it is safe:
evening and dawn,
dowsing water where
others find none.

Armored things.
Scaled things.
Venomous things.
Things with teeth
and claws and
a will to live;

cactus blossoms
exploding into color
in the dark, proving
the best beauty blooms
for itself.

We must become
the desert creatures,
finding what we can
to sustain ourselves;

the dry times teach us
thirst is both a lack
and a purpose

Noumenon or *having my breast implants removed*

So, Dr. Aesthetics,
open me up.
unbeauty me. I tire
of prying lust leeches
from my skin.

Slice here: grasp
elephantine
dew drops. Pinch, pluck
away plastic sex appeal —
breasts crumple, collapse:
raisins in the sun.

shiny, writhing black pearls
drop from skin to floor, soon
replaced by blooming ladybug carapaces
and a deflated sense of self

I peel away the layers of posturing:
the jig, amble and lisp;
flay open my chest
in the name of authenticity

or something like it until
all that remains

is empty, puckered skin.

David Havird

David Havird has other recent poems in *The American Journal of Poetry*, *The Hopkins Review*, *Literary Matters*, and *Literary Imagination*. He is the author of two collections, *Map Home* (2013) and *Penelope's Design* (2010), which won the Robert Phillips Poetry Chapbook Prize. He teaches at Centenary College of Louisiana.

Crown of Thorns

A tree up from our broken reality ... Keeping faith.
— Rolf Jacobsen (trans. Roger Greenwald)

When we got down, there ambled toward us
a large white dog with a blue bandana
in place of a collar, and one of the children
had to stoop and *ooh*, her face
in its one only face, and it —

it wagged its tail. But once we'd assembled,
toed the length of the platform, its master,
bleached-blond Mohawk, bomber jacket,
combat boots with red laces, and something
whisky-brown in an Evian bottle, *oohed*,
his face in ours. He snarled and jabbed the air.

He strutted, flung his middle finger up,
then paused. "Don't even glance his way,"
I whispered to Trina, whose eyes were tearing.
That gesture, did he have it right?
he asked in English. A chorus of nods,

that one child mouthing *oui*. He spat
viciously onto the tracks, then off he marched
to an exit, the white dog trotting behind him.
Our stop was Trocadéro, the summit's view
of the Eiffel Tower sparkling. Later,
after we had toured the Catacombs,

we pictured the Métro as shelf on shelf
of skulls. Down there, I told the children,
I'd heard again as through the broken grin
of skulls Coach Pinkerton snarling, "You think"
(we boys who huddled on wooden benches),

"you're all so young" (in our fresh uniforms),
"you're going to live forever, but me,
I know I'm not. Every morning
the man in the mirror whispers *You're going to die*"
(each of us huddling more deeply
into himself), down where stone dark can't tell

if finger bones or roots have seized it, roots
"planted in our humiliation," up
from which there burgeons over the earth a tree,
its crown amid the stars. So down we went,
and there was a dog, if only a one-headed mutt

whose master it was that bared his teeth and snarled,
blond Mohawk, red-laced boots, who flipped us off.
Then up, as though we scaled that tree,
to skitter along a lamplit street
as though along a shimmering branch,
the skyline prickling with thorns of light.

Thin Disguise

The ferry was bobbing and creaking.
Head bobbing, I pictured the rocker at home,
also my mother as she must have pictured herself
when she and her sisters were sorting Grandmother's things:
a new mother there at her mother's
rocking her colicky boy. Why else had she wanted it,
oak with a drab upholstered seat and back?
Its creaking put me to sleep,
she shrugged, as nothing else could.

I slept my first night through on the island,
on sea-legs staggered to breakfast, a lavish affair
conjured up by a witch in black leggings.
Was it the apron or was she acquiring a paunch,
this Circe, behind whom sauntered
in place of a panther a calico cat?
Sleeveless her black knit top. On her bronze arms
I fixed the ravenous gaze of a wayfaring man.

At dinner I hog an outdoor table for four.
I slide the knife along the spine of my fish
while eying a couple who've swayed downhill
as if they strayed from a revel. She's wooing,

this blonde with short shorts on
and a blouse that slips from a shoulder
or rises to show her navel whenever she motions,
out from between the menu boards
maybe the calico's kitten,
while her young man, gripping with one hand
a bottle of wine by the neck, picks at his whiskers,
the tourist's first beard, with his other, and what I feel
on my new face, a breeze
from the harbor, where my beard was
is like cold fingertips, the sinking sun's, which read
as through a thick disguise a bald-faced lie;
and when the sun, despite its lens of cloud,
finds on my leathery wrist,
right as I lift with the blade white flakes of meat,
white hairs amid the brown like feathery fish bones,
I picture in place of her feverish boy
a graybeard without any beeswax to stopper his ears,
a bone-heaped beach in place of the lap of his mother.

Meryl Natchez

Meryl Natchez' most recent book is a bilingual volume of translations from the Russian: *Poems From the Stray Dog Café: Akhmatova, Mandelstam and Gumilev*. She is co-translator of *Tadeusz Borowski: Selected Poems*. Her book of poems, *Jade Suit*, appeared in 2001. Her work has appeared in *The American Journal of Poetry*, ZYZZYVA, *The Pinch Literary Review*, *Atlanta Review*, *Lyric*, *The Moth*, *Comstock Review*, and many others. She is on the board of Marin Poetry Center.

Gem Stone

Years of drips in just one spot
scar the worn enamel of the sink
one drip at a time
until the powdered glass unfuses its mineral
bond, laying bare the iron beneath,
one black star of use.
So, after forty years your essence
reveals itself: familiar, flawed,
hardened by wear — the one I fell for
before I knew anything, glove
to my hand, derringer in my pocket,
sand in my oyster, four decades
polished to pearl.

Skull of a Small Mammal

The bleached skull sits on the kitchen counter,
provenance unknown.
The teeth could make a necklace
for a Pomo bride — their points delicate
and deadly, a reminder that
the untamed continues to exist
despite the microwave,
the Dispose-all. The savage lurks
in the web above the sink, the dying
fly, the primitive flash I feel
when you leave the good knife unwashed.
I could almost use it on you,
you, the one I love most
when I am able to think,
when my fangs retract a moment,
when my fur remembers your fingers.

The Ways I See You

the flash of the hook
when I rise to the bait

      how your eyebrows give the joke away

in your baseball cap
and championship t-shirt

      you with the facts, doing the math

the hard set
your mouth can take

      on the treadmill at the gym, talking to yourself

over breakfast
reading to me from the Times

      your willingness to try even swing-dance, even yoga

full black beard
pounding abalone

      gray stubble no place particular to go

in a suit with a mic
at our daughter's wedding

      your shoulder against a dolly under something heavy

on I-5, on 880
talking, missing the exit

      your hands over the sink

on the keyboard
with hammer or X-ACTO or pen

      the current I stand in, its surge and drag

your face in the mirror next to mine
day after day forgetting to really look at you
as if you would be here forever

Roy Mash

Roy Mash is the author of *Buyer's Remorse* (Cherry Grove, 2014). His poems have appeared in *AGNI Online*, *Atlanta Review*, *Barrow Street*, *The Evansville Review*, *Nimrod*, *Poetry East*, *RHINO*, and *River Styx* among others. He is the recipient of the Atlanta Review International Publication Award. Roy Mash has also served as a board member of Marin Poetry Center.

Two Saints of Clarity

During the invasion of Syracuse,
or so the story goes, Archimedes
was sitting in the road engrossed
with a problem he'd scratched into the dust,
and pleaded with the centurion
who'd swaggered up, hot to run
him through, to be spared a brief
minute only, to scribble out the proof.

Antoine Lavoisier, so it is said,
the night before he was to be beheaded
took tea and attended to his hair,
having arranged with the executioner
to hold the still-thinking thing up to the crowd,
that his confederate, the celebrated
mathematician Lagrange, might count his blinks,
and so settle a fine point of science.

So what if the story-tellers lied?
Reason loves its legends too, fables that
inflame, like the tales of these saints
of clarity, on whose dying faces
appeared no rouge of adoration or
piety, transfiguration or prayer—
just pure curiosity, peering out,
unperturbed, above the rushing blood.

Hardly Lord Jim

I was the one
who got on all fours
behind chubby
and unsuspecting Fred
when Mike
shoved him in the chest
and he fell backward
over me
while Donny laughed.

That was it, as I remember.
Nobody went to the hospital.
There was no blood.
The grass
absorbed the fall,
most likely.

So
here I am
at the other end
of my life,
hardly Lord Jim,
but still
unable to put out
of my mind
me there
on all fours.

Revolving Sunglass Display

There is in each of us
a silo of desire
that circles on itself
and lurches with each turn.

It sports a dozen styles
of debonair, of dash
and breeze, and if it could
would make Marcello
Mastroiannis of us all.

But here in this local
corner store it's a funny,
studded, rickety beast,
blind for all its eyes
and miles from any beach.

Thomas Centolella

Thomas Centolella is the author of four collections of poetry: *Terra Firma*, *Lights & Mysteries*, *Views from along the Middle Way*, and *Almost Human* (2017), which won the Dorset Prize from Tupelo Press. His honors include the American Book Award, the Lannan Literary Award, the California Book Award, the Northern California Book Award, and publication in the National Poetry Series. He is a former Wallace Stegner Fellow at Stanford University where he studied poetry with Denise Levertov and fiction with Grace Paley. His work has appeared in numerous magazines and anthologies and on NPR's *The Writer's Almanac*.

Wake

A sweetness steals through the mind,
lingering hint of flower or fragrant bark…

A thousand miles off the African coast
Napoleon would die with a locket of pressed violets

gathered from Josephine's grave,
remnants of bloom to remind him

of the intoxicating wake she'd leave across a room:
sillage, you said was the French word for it, intoxicated yourself

by the very idea, which is why I was surprised to learn
how taken you were by the unscented

smell of my body: your words a sudden turn
toward the tender, a trace escaping the shuttered room,

the island shore of your exiled heart:
a sudden remark as sweet as it was slight,

lovely then in its passing, and lovely now
as it passes again.

Pietà

Well before the end
she was little more
than the bones beneath her skin
her mouth open as if to implore
the pain to release her from its ceaseless grip

And when at last it did
her onlyborn asked the nurses
to remove the needle of the useless drip
and leave him alone with her
Whatever grievances whatever curses

had been lining up to have their say
would have to wait   He removed the shroud
of the unruffled sheet and bent to lift
what was left of her   wizened cloud
of the bitter and sweet   and lowered the two of them

into the nearest chair   And there
in his lap is where
she lay at rest
while the first snow wandered in every direction
light as dust

The Happiness Test

They had me sit in a comfortable chair.
Put the electrodes on me. Dimmed the lights.
Instructed me to "think of nothing," something they knew
was easier said than done and I knew was not impossible.
But before going there, I had to go through the children
drinking and bathing in water a sewer rat wouldn't touch,
I had to go through the bald eagle poisoned to death by lead,
and then the videos gone viral: the unarmed brothers, going about
their business, choked out or shot on the spot; the orange-clad
    journalists
and their severed heads; the refugee on the beach who didn't
    make it
past the age of three. When the plutocrat exhorted the demagogue
to interfere with the election, I had to push through the miasma
of the not-fair-and-never-will-be, nudging the better angels of our
    nature
for some better direction. By then, nothing began to look pretty
    good to me.

But this was just part one of the happiness test.
They had me lie down on the patient table (was I not patient
    enough
and trying my best?) and slid me into the scanner. Are you ready?
came a soothing voice. Then commenced the images, a flow

of steady goodnesses: loving mom and dad; a lavish buffet; sex
in the woods, on the beach, on a blanket of grass. And then:
belly dancer, Beaujolais, supermoon over Yosemite.
And, at the last, a stack of money (always money, aka
filthy lucre). Later they showed me how my brain had lit up
like the Northern Lights and the Southern Lights, and even
        some lights
they still didn't have a name for — all aglow from wants
and likes and must-haves and love love loves —

so I asked them if that meant I had passed the happiness test.
What do you think? they replied, aping their colleagues
the shrinks. I said I thought I had some way to go,
though I had my moments. They looked at me like I was daft.
Might daft be some kind of happy? I thought. What, pray tell,
is happiness anyway? Then one of them said, You're
        overthinking it,
aren't you. And we laughed and laughed and laughed.

Education

I sat on the taking-forever bus, my pale hands in my lap,
a casual observer of my own demise. Pain this great,
you seek diversion: I went straight to the ad
for higher education, the chance for advancement,
then felt a wan affection for the unsmiling child
who stared at me as if she knew
I had come as far as I ever would.
The pain might not have been greater
than anyone else's, but it forced me to consider
it might never end. It forced me
into a quiet and a stillness I imagine
is reserved for the gods. There might have been
genial chatter among the passengers,
there might have been a soft breath
of air from an open window — I couldn't say,
I was so close to the end. Pleasure, I remembered,
was the absence of pain, and pleasure had decided
it was no longer my friend. There might have been
the thought of friends, the ones I would tell my story to,
the story of a fire somewhere in my bowels,
where the Bible says mercy resides, but this fire

a nonbeliever in everything but itself, a far cry from respite
or the purifying, this fire. Still, there might have been
cause to believe I'd come through this unscathed —
I don't remember. What I do remember
is that like any of the stricken I looked for reasons,
the kind that favored consolation over explanation.
But reasons were like riders: slow to arrive,
lost to the clarities beyond the windows,
ignoring me as they stepped back
into the vivid world, while I could only abide
in the agony of my unknowing. Even now
I can't tell you that much about the pain, the unending
depth of it, the sear and scorch and despair of it.
When I go back to that day it's only the quiet
and the stillness that endure. That
and the waiting, while the fates debated
their favorite subject: whether one more mortal
should be put out of his misery, or if misery — contrary
to all human inclination and comprehension —
might somehow in the end prove useful.

Lisa Rappoport

Photo by Bobbe Besold

Lisa Rappoport is a letterpress printer, book artist, book designer and poet, creating artist's books and poetry broadsides under the imprint Littoral Press. Rappoport teaches book arts workshops throughout the Bay Area. Her work is in national and international collections and has been included in such surveys as *500 Handmade Books* and *1000 Artists' Books*. She has two books of poetry: *Words Fail {Me}*, an artist's book (2014) and *Aftermaths/Figments*, a chapbook from Etherdome (2009). Her poetry appeared most recently in the anthologies *The 2017 Richmond Anthology of Poetry* and *Pluto: New Horizons for a Lost Horizon* (North Atlantic Books, 2015), and the journal *Caesura* (2016).

When I Was a Beauty Queen

I was dying to taste my own pillowy lips,
which looked ever ready to bestow a blow job;
I wondered if I'd be able to blow myself.
Self-tickling doesn't work but since you can excite
yourself, auto-kissing seemed dimly possible.
You can smell your own excretions but can
you taste your flesh? It's like a fish knowing
how wet the water is on a particular morning.

All those millions of fans with voracious eyes,
their clammy skins and racing pulses,
left me unstirred. Many called me icy, aloof,
as if I had any relation at all to those *others*,
as if we dwelt in the same universe.
What hurt was the distance between me and me,
the body I could neither escape nor possess,
the scent I couldn't perceive, the responses
I could set in motion, alone or partnered,
only by fantasizing someone else, someone
infinitely alluring, some one the only one,
the only me.

When I Was a Boy

I was afraid of the girls: their cliques and all
that gossiping made me sick for them all.

Their willingness to wear dresses
showed they bought into the rhetoric and all.

Worthwhile activities like climbing trees or bicycling
were severely hampered by such icky folderol.

Submitting to unfair constraints was a sign of insanity.
To those girls, my refusal was cryptic above all.

I never had an imaginary friend, only an imagined
boy self. Girls got the short end of the stick is all.

I tested my physical courage all the time,
while fearing my own destiny, private, public: all.

The stirrings of sex made me abandon boyness.
But I never betrayed the flame that flickers at all.

Heaped with protective coals, it smolders on and on.
Lisa — Jerry, your life emerges from an alembic. Fire is all.

When I Was Human

All that wanting
swallowed my life —
it was a boa and marmot
situation

The me that was the boa
was insatiable

Marmot-me squeaked its protest
but succumbed
over and over

Even wanting the wanting
to stop
availed not

At last
we swallowed
our own tail

Jane Shlensky

Jane Shlensky has poetry in a number of magazines and anthologies, including *Writer's Digest*, *Pinesong*, *Kakalak*, *Southern Poetry Anthology: NC*, and *Poetry Market*. NC Poetry Society has twice nominated her poems for a Pushcart, and her short fiction and nonfiction pieces were finalists in Press 53, Doris Betts, Rose Post, and Thomas Wolfe contests. Jane's chapbook *Barefoot on Gravel* (2016) is published by Finishing Line Press.

The Poetics of Gentle Fencing

We eye the fence discouraged by what we see. The posts and split rails are choked with poison oak twisted among honeysuckle vines, the fence line punctuated by the occasional cedar tree or blackberry brier, the top strand of barbed wire swaybacked under the weight. "Ain't this a fine how d'ya do?" Wilbur says, no more willing to tackle this cleanup than I am, but I'm the designated starter in all our jobs, always have been, so I heft the clippers and tug on my gloves.

"The old lady — Miss Annie — wants what she wants, and she's willing to pay. Best get to it." Sometimes all Wil needs is a first step and then he's on his way and can outwork ten men. It's getting him to take that first step that is always the challenge.

"Yeah, yeah. But look it," he says, "these vines are muscled like trees near the roots. Them clippers won't do. Plus this is prob'ly full of snakes and bees and all manner of bugs." He kicks at a thick cedar trunk overwhelmed with vines. "And honey! Did she even factor in how this kind of destruction to honeysuckle will affect honey production this year? Web Vance's bees are bound to be drawn to the vines over here. Bet she didn't ask him about it." I smirk and shake my head; he's on a roll. "And another thing — this is a big job. Must be half a mile of fencing overrun like this."

"That's the point, I think. She says it's ruining the fence. Her husband, Zeb Marshall — do you remember him chasing us out of his apples when we were kids?—paid top dollar to build that fence who-knows-when but nobody can even see it with all this vegetation." I'm already sweating just arguing with him.

"Vegetation, yeah. This'll take forever, cutting and pulling and burning." He slaps his ball cap against his leg a few times and wipes his face with his handkerchief. "We could just burn it off," he says, studying the length of fence. I wait to see if he figures it out while he paces and pulls out a bird's nest a wren just vacated. After a few minutes, I say, "Wood fence?" and lift my eyebrows meaningfully.

"Oh. Yeah. Well, seems like if Zeb was so keen on seeing the fence, he shouldn't 'a let the vines take it? Looks like he'd a put in some effort early on."

"Well, I suspect he was busy dying most of the time this thicket's been growing. She's a widow — Mrs. Marshall. He died slow with the cancer. She wants to put it back to rights as a kind of tribute to him. Said he couldn't stand to look out the window from that hospital bed set up in their living room and see it getting overrun and him not able to change that. I guess he talked about it a good bit before he went." Wil looks disgruntled. It's hard to argue with the dead. "That's what she said. I guess we could ask if she wants us to leave some for her to breathe, something sweet for the bees. Nothing smells better than honeysuckle on a mild night. I read about some feller making ice cream from honeysuckle, how he had to milk a gazillion of the blossoms for that little drop of sweetness just to make a gallon of the stuff. He must charge a ton for one little taste. I would."

Wil flails among the vines looking peeved at birds and bees scattering from the mess. I start snipping stems down to the thick parts while he pulls the runners into piles laying them in the pasture like garlands.

"Better separate the poison oak from the rest. We can't burn that or it'll blister our lungs. Happened to Burt Metz a few years ago — had to get shots for it for weeks."

"Good grief," mumbles Wil. "Like it ain't a big enough pain in the ass. We'll need to haul these runners off so we don't set the pasture on fire with 'em."

"Just thought I'd save us some time later on. I tell you what, Wil, let's roll 'em up and tie 'em off. We can make honey-suckle vine wreathes like they have at the craft fair. We can sell 'em."

"Craft fair," he says, eyeing me like he does when he's try-ing to push my buttons. "Elvin, whatever in the hell are you talking about? Now you're a crafty craftsman? Painting little whatsits and gluing on rickrack?" He grins at the image he paints, knowing I'm not blessed with fine motor skills.

"Ah, Jenny made me go with her last year to sell her quilts, and you wouldn't believe some of the stuff that constitutes crafts. Everything from crocheted fruit cozies to hand-made paper. People pay perfectly good money for seasonal wreaths for their doors."

"Like how much?"

"I don't know. Depends on size, I reckon. Twenty to fifty dollars with froufrou on 'em."

Wil straightens, looks down the long fence line, and whistles long and low. "Whew, man. We're looking at a fortune here.

I'll get some twine tomorrow. Today I'll tie up vines with vines."

"Now you're talking, buddy. Old folks used to use grape vines and all sorts of vines to make baskets — do you remember that? I remember my Gram soaking runners to make them pliable." My head is suddenly full of her wiry hands and nimble fingers braiding and weaving as if her hands are not aware she's half blind. I imagine my thick fingers trying to fashion a basket anyone would have and can't see that ever happening, these hands good for big course work and heavy lifting. Wil and I work side by side, grunting and cursing the tangles, talking to wrens and sparrows that fly into our faces from inside the thicket. Wil hates destroying animal habitats. He pulls nests from the bramble and puts them gently on the ground in a circle of vines, like a little village for birds. He's sensitive about bothering animals that do no harm, like St. Francis of the woodlands, a garland on his head, birds dripping off him, a black snake wound around his neck like a scarf, field mice and ground hogs nestled at his feet. The image makes me smile and seeing it, he smiles too like he can read my mind.

"Wouldn't it be half funny if the only thing holding up the fence was the vines?" he says.

"That would be a sad irony," I tell him, "but we'd still get paid."

He snorts and works on, wrapping runners and piling poison oak with other trash, but he's jumpy and agitated. "Irony! Ev, why you always knowing stuff."

"I don't know what you mean. How would I unknow stuff?"

"No, don't get witty and make it worse. Words, plans, ideas, like that. Where do you get that?"

"Wil, I don't understand what you mean, man. What's got you bothered?"

He's silent for thirty minutes or more, working along steady and calm, so I figure he's done when he says, "I'd give near anything to be a smart man. To know things and have ideas, but I'm just big, dumb, and awkward. Women don't go for that, so's you know."

I've known Wil Hollinger my whole life, and he's never been anything but big and slow and steady as a plow horse. He ain't mean or nasty talking or pushy. He could do some real damage if he ever got in a fight — hell, his hands are like shovels — but he's not inclined to fight. He's one of the best men I know and I tell him so. Sometimes a man needs to know what he's worth to his friends. He looks pleased and embarrassed but keeps working so he won't have to look me in the eye, but I get to thinking about his definition of smart. "Wil, I have more ideas in a minute than I can execute in a year. Do you know how frustrating that can be?"

"I reckon we make a good team. One brain, one brawn."

"Hell, yeah! And women? At least the kind of women we'd want to end up with, want a solid man, seems to me, some-body who can work and laugh and love 'em good and carry through on just a few ideas over a lifetime."

"Like building a board fence for one old horse." Marshall's old bay stands a few yards away watching us work as if it's the most fun she's had in years, and it probably is.

"Yeah, something like that."

Wil looks across at the Marshall house up a slight hill in oak and apple shade. "You know, I always heard Old Man Marshall was hard on his missus, crabby and bossy like. Kept her on a tight leash." He spits and pulls a grass straw to chew on. "I reckon she loved him just the same. Enough to stay, anyway."

"I guess so."

He stands considering, working the straw in his teeth. "Maybe he was like this mess here to her. Mostly honeysuckle with a little poison oak, all tangled up together around something solid, something that could be beautiful with a little work."

In a thousand years, I'd not have said that. My God, he's a poet! I reach to cup his neck in my hand and give him a shake. "You ain't so dumb, Wil. Not so dumb at all," I tell him.

Emily Wolahan

Owen Brown

The poet and the artist of The Fieldwork Scroll

Emily Wolahan is the author of the poetry collection *Hinge*. Her poems have been published in *Boston Review*, *Volt*, DIAGRAM, *Tinderbox*, and others. She won the 2016 Loraine Williams Poetry Prize and the Unclassifiables Contest. She is Senior Editor at Two Lines Press, Editor of *JERRY Magazine*, and lives in San Francisco. She is currently an Affiliate Artist at the Headlands Center for the Arts.

Owen Brown received his artistic training at Yale and at California College of Arts, where he painted under Philip Morseberger and Jack Mendenhall. His works are in collections in Asia and the United States. He has exhibited widely in this country, and he has been published in media as varied as the *San Francisco Chronicle*, A5, Paragon, and the Society for Art Publications of the Americas.

The Fieldwork Scroll

The Fieldwork Scroll is a poetic and visual response to one of the starkest realities of our contemporary era: the global migration and diaspora of millions of refugees.

Created by artist Owen Brown and poet Emily Wolahan, the Fieldwork Scroll is a poem and painting that move together through a landscape of violence, loss, and the contemplation of both. Wolahan's poem meditates on a feeling of displacement and uncertainty, anchored only by family, in this case the speaker's son. Brown's painting, at times figurative, at times abstract, makes visual that sense of displacement and violence. Blending color and line, the painting depicts explosion, water, and flight, summoning aspects of a refugee journey and the helplessness of being an observer.

The Fieldwork Scroll unfolds experiences of terror, travel, and dislocation through a journey that does not finish here, but continues for people displaced and in danger.

The scroll is twenty-
five feet long, printed
on translucent duralar
plastic. Eight copies have been
produced.

Brown and Wolahan began their collaboration
with a recognition of the need for compassion over
paralyzing empathy, lyric response over tweetable platitudes.
Harkening back to the ancient in its form, the result is a
hybrid piece of art and writing suited for the contemporary
world embraced by the unknown.

The scroll is represented in the following pages by six
panels or sections of the scroll. These selections present the
beginning and end of the scroll and four portions between.
While in the original scroll the poem is integrated with the
imagery, our representation extracts the words and places
them onto facing pages. Neither all of the artwork nor all of
the poem is presented here.

1. "a card home"

Write a card home
about the Brooklyn Bridge burning,
quite a fire, no injuries.
The neighbor's brownstone explodes —
pushes glass off our windows.
We skip going to work today —
our first flu of the year.
Instead, routine holds.
Rector street. Sirens come but no telling
from where. A sense that fire is in everything.
Every object has potential; bricks
tumble off Red Hook West,
scatter dents on the cars below.

We outline the town, house in it,
and this room. We sit in a leather swivel chair
and wait. You'll know the switch
when you see it — and what it can do.
              The idea light could explode.

We enter another room we created,
reach for the switch. On a computer screen:
four plaster walls, a wooden floor, no ceiling.

2. "house, town"

house, town — The room
until there is no room —
it lies around our feet.
We take our equipment
back home with us.
They continue to win.

We throw our hands in the air;
They fly away from our bodies.

We crowd around the broken earth,
legless table, pock-marked
soldier, and brindled dog;
the half-wrapped infant (how could
they have ever lived?).
They ought to be different
but they are not.
Dust settles on everything:
angles of broken stone, eyelashes.
The boy's smooth cheek firm
like my son pressing against me.
Was it a surprise —
a child's backpack crushed
and tossed to the side.

3. "with a child"

The mother with a child that won't move.
We are running out of the smoke.
The child refuses to move.
An emergency light flashes yellow
on the child's face. The mother
can't carry the child.
An emergency lights yellow.
The child won't move.

empty as in destroyed therefore removed
a town emptied of its people
empty as in not empty at all

6. "empty as in no place empty"

empty as in no place empty
as if filled with a past
but upon looking there is
nothing to behold empty as in thread
the thread is one that we follow
My son drags
a line of chalk behind him
so I will have a route to follow. empty as in spent
as in looking at you
across the street
we may lock eyes but my
thoughts
are emptied

As in, there is never a direct account;
it was all so long ago, why not release it —
His paleness, he is empty of color.
Here's a page
the date you're looking for,
direct access,
direct route to a moment.
In telling, a sparrow tapping
on air before it releases its trill.

7. "as in occupied"

as in occupied
rendered empty and ridden
with holes
out seeps the black line
pipeline or underline or through line
I occupy each letter left behind
each word rendered
empty the line breaks
compassion or testimony?
I reach out my fist, unfurl it.
We walk aware
of instruments of record
capturing every move.
Photograph the moving water
with our memories. Carry our things
in plastic bags.

A street sweeper says
the walk down the coast to Pula
will take a while. On our feet, flip flops.

The sea breaks blue in half.
We have lost places, people —
that's not news.
We swap our post for outpost
until each is vague,
like a mossed edge of the twig
meant to decompose.
No one calls you by your name.

Andy Plumb/Selena Anne Shephard

Andy Plumb/Selena Anne is a writer/photographer who has created three books of poems, prose, photographs, and collages: *Doll Hearts*, *Bootleg Poems*, and *Poems from Big Pink*. Andy/Selena enjoy exploring gender possibilities in a variety of ways, and also like walking, birding, Contra dancing, big trees, and the songs of Leonard Cohen (to name one of many musical influences).

be
   *h*er
      *n*ow

You dress to kill.
Cross your legs with reckless abandon.
But you are of two minds. Four hearts.
Love's a fool's awakening
a stark reminder of our fragility.
The moon, a sliver, yet you marry anyway,
to a distant light
on an unknowing night.

I've come out in layers since I was 16
and still I am not quite there.
There, that place where I can wear my mask
and the illusion's no delusion.
Where I'll stroll out in shocking pink
neither dress nor pants
a sheath perhaps
or a silken scarf spiraling.

     If you unravel
          my brain traces of
             lace will remain.

she painted me away

She painted me away
to a field
where Wyeth the younger lay
naked stark
to Whitman's touch
        and Ginsberg's gaze
She painted me away

She painted me away
into a block of urgent red
        where Rothko raged
and Berryman slipped closer to the edge
She painted me away

She painted me away
into Pollock swift surges
James Dean in close pursuit
        shiny new cars up in flames
She painted me away

She painted me away
to Virginia's room
where we slept
with sirens in our head
        and stones in our pockets
She painted me away

Deborah Buchanan

Deborah Buchanan is a poet who has taught creative writing at Pacific NW College of Art, written book and poetry reviews online, and in print publications. She volunteers with Open Hearts Open Minds leading dialogue and writing groups in correctional institutions. Her work has appeared in *Squaw Valley Review*, *Tule Review*, *Cloudbank*, *Event*, *West Marin Review,* and *Artemis*. She collaborates with the composer Lisa Marsh, her poems sung as lyrics in concert and on the CD *Along the Road*.

Step Forward Step Back

In an open space
a thin line
the horizon.
You walk towards me,
we recognize each other,
smile, look into the other's eyes,
then with deft movement
you reach across your chest
and open it to me,
a corporeal door swung ajar.
Nothing bloody, nothing fleshy
as I look inside, nothing.
I am you, you say,
your smile covering distance,
erasing peculiarities.
As our eyes continue to hold
you step closer and

with the same suppleness
open my torso: chest, stomach,
fluttering breath. You are me.
Still we watch, space
streaming around us.
A chirrup from the birds
in an unseen tree.
Quiet.
Your eyes.
We are nothing, you say,
We are transparent.
Transparent the line of my arm.
Nothing the shape of your mouth.
Nothing the touch on my arm.
Transparent my fingers to your face,
your lips evanescent in the startling blue.

Darkening

I prayed to your fingertips,
a pale, translucent pink,
so small and barely curved,

that they would one day
feel the wavering
greenness of grass,
touch the incandescence
of flame,
or cup themselves
to hold
the cold rush of
a mountain freshet.

I prayed to your fingertips
that I might kiss
their shape, held
to my warm mouth.

I prayed
as the dusky color
of eggplant
crept in,
claiming your fingers,
and Death answered
my prayers with
his own indigo.

Michael Jones

Michael Jones has taught in Oakland, California, public schools since 1990. His poetry appears widely in journals, including *Atlanta Review*, *Beloit Poetry Journal*, *Confrontation*, and *DMQ Review*, and in a chapbook, *Moved* (Kattywompus, 2016).

Studying The Dying Gaul

"Hella nistic? That's hella weird!"
my student laughs. Philistine, I think,
but that begs questions: whose story?
What fight? Whose Palestine?

I smile and say, "Not hella-, it's Hellen-, it's Greek,"
begging questions I think I can answer.
The silence enclosing my first thought
echoes both the glowing marble
and the nameless warrior it captures.

Whose naked leaning into death provokes
my student, one who hears gunfire day and night,
as shell-shocked as teens along the Jordan.
He looks away, then looks again. I do the same.
The dying Gaul will not lie down. What do I teach?

Greek Wins Gold At Olympics

Athens, 2004

Her fallen fatherland's mother tongue
requires translation; the force
gathered in her cry does not. Before
a world whose rivalries are far
from brave or new, in triumph
indifferent to grace and hoarse
with battle's candor, she raves,
For Greece! For fuckin' Greece!

Man With Back to Avenue, December

He gazes across the city
to the hills from which coyotes
venture, temperate scrubland's
snowless solstice dusted
with the sun's own wintriness.

Maybe you know the feeling.
Or maybe you feel it's nothing,
trivia; but a trivium
is a place where three roads
meet, and Oedipus came
to just such a crossing.

In the dust of intentions,
in the midst of trivia,
invention's avenues
present the unforeseen.

James Tipton

James Tipton is the author of *Annette Vallon, A Novel of the French Revolution* (HarperCollins, 2008), based on the true story of William Wordsworth's great love. It was a *San Francisco Chronicle* Bestseller and a Barnes & Noble Discover Pick. Tipton has also published poetry and short fiction; recently, "The Vampire of Edinburgh" and "Shiva's Eye" in *Alfred Hitchcock Mystery Magazine* and "The Lieutenant at Dachau" (based on his father's experience at the Dachau War Crimes Trials) in the literary magazine *Blue Unicorn*. Gary Snyder called Tipton's book of poetry, *Sacred Places*, "keen, taut, and skillful."

Movies

Coleman's Daughter, Los Angeles, 1936

Every Saturday they did their morning chores then went to the movies and stayed all afternoon. Gary Cooper was their favorite. Others were wonderful — Ronald Colman in *Tale of Two Cities*, for instance, and he almost had their last name, if only he hadn't forgotten to put the e in — Ronald Colman was stunning with his smooth voice and noble character, but it was Gary Cooper who kept them all day at the cinema.

After they saw *The Virginian* for the first time, they took out their meatloaf sandwiches wrapped in wax paper and poured their thermos of hot chocolate, sharing the cup, and waited while the movie theatre filled up again. There was something about how quiet he was and how utterly you could trust him. He was taller than the other stars and maybe not as charming, but then you could not rely on the others the way you could rely on Cooper.

People called him Coop, so Elizabeth and her sister Carolyn called him Coop, as if they were his friends. They felt that they were his friends. They liked his quiet, even slow way of talking, and how he seemed to think about everything before he spoke. He wanted to make sure he got it right, for every word out of his mouth was the intractable truth, and he would stand by it to the death.

For other stars, words were cheap; you could bandy about words to show how charming or smart or in command you were, but Coop, he would chew over each one and when he finally said them, he would never take them back. Their president, Franklin Delano Roosevelt, used language like that. It was more flowing, of course, because he gave speeches, but every word counted. You could count on his words to mean something. Their daddy used language like that — not too many words but everyone listened to every one of them.

Elizabeth and Carolyn sat in the balcony and sipped their hot chocolate. They didn't have the money for popcorn or ice cream and didn't care. This was far better. They didn't mind the looks of others as the sisters ate their sandwiches. They were glad they had them. They had seen the men in the long lines waiting for some watery soup and a slice of hard bread. They had seen the lines of men waiting when just one position of clerk opened at a store. They were happy their daddy had a job, even if he didn't always sell as much as he wanted to and even if he had to take orders from managers when he himself used to tell many other men what to do. Daddy didn't say much, like Coop, about the things that bothered him, but Elizabeth knew he had many burdens and that it was part of her job to make life easy for him when he came home. She couldn't cook, but she loved waiting on Daddy when he came home. She brought his drink that Mama mixed. She brought him his paper and sometimes a picture she had drawn. Mama never asked him about his day when he came home. He had his chair, and he had his peace and quiet.

Another movie star came along, different from the others, and totally different from Coop. It wasn't the glorious King of Hollywood in *It Happened One Night.* It was a young buccaneer with long hair and shoulders even broader than Coop's — a man who made them all want to be pirates. His men were pirates for a good cause, for they had been terribly wronged — sold into slavery by their own government. And Peter Blood — for that was the pirate's name — had simply been honoring his sacred code as a doctor.

So much of the world was now in a kind of slavery, like the men in the long lines, her father trying to sell, day in and day out, when he, like Dr. Blood, had once had a thriving business of his own and a high position in their town. But Captain Blood led them out of slavery and onto the high seas. Captain Blood reaped revenge upon the plunderers, plundering them in turn, and, in his heart, in his eyes, you could tell he was gentle and as honest as Coop. But unlike Coop, who was always alone, Captain Blood culled a following. "Look at the sails that are carrying us to freedom!" he'd shout, or something like that, and everyone in the theatre wanted to follow Captain Blood. Elizabeth and Carolyn had a slight disagreement about the new star, Errol Flynn. While remaining true to Coop, Elizabeth wanted also to acknowledge that Flynn was the most dashing man in the world. Carolyn would have none of it.

There were occasional Saturdays when they didn't go to the movies — nothing new was playing or it was all gangster movies — and on these days the sisters went on skating journeys to the sea. They roller skated through Griffith Park, waved to the doorman of the Biltmore Hotel who knew them by now and waved back, skated down the bumpy road where there was no sidewalk through the fields west of Hollywood, went fast by the steps of UCLA to impress any college students, and on to the sea. Elizabeth, being the oldest, carried in a knapsack onion sandwiches she'd made that morning and a thermos of lemonade and orange juice, from oranges she had squeezed from the tree in their small backyard.

They picnic'd on the sand and watched the waves and waded and screamed deliciously when the cool water splashed above their knees. They shooed away gulls wanting scraps, gathered shells, and noticed the handsome lifeguard. They heard a clever young man playing a ukulele and singing the song Katherine Hepburn and Cary Grant had sung to calm the leopard in *Bringing Up Baby*. The man had about half a dozen pretty girls about him, all adoring him and laughing at things he said. Elizabeth and Carolyn thought the girls very silly and, as the sun was beginning to lay a path on the water, put the thermos in the knapsack and headed back.

They were tired and took the Red Line part of the way, and Elizabeth sat with her elbows on her knees and her head in her hands. When they resumed skating, Los Angeles seemed a hundred miles wide. They were in Hollywood, not far from Grumman's Chinese, where they knew *The Charge of the Light Brigade* was premiering that night, when they saw a silver Daimler parked in the shade of a palm tree. The sidewalk they were skating on led straight past the big car. The back door was open onto a strip of lawn by the curb, and Elizabeth saw polished shoes on the running board and shiny black trousers under the door. A hand with gold cuff links at its wrist flicked ash from a cigarette. Then a head leaned forward.

His elbows rested on his knees and the man held his head in his hands. The girls skated by. Elizabeth glanced at his carefully combed hair, and for a moment he lifted his eyes. She almost lost her balance but continued and stopped suddenly at the corner. Carolyn almost bumped into her.

"What are you doing?" her little sister asked.

"Did you see who that was?"

"The drunk tycoon by the car?"

"Don't talk like that. He wasn't drunk. He was just tired, like us. And you wouldn't talk like that if you had seen who it was."

"All right, who?"

"You won't believe it."

"I probably won't."

"Errol Flynn."

"Errol Flynn? Hah! Why would he be sitting in his car with the door open? He would be at some big party."

"Well, why don't you go ask him?"

"Me? I'm not the one who thinks she just skated by a movie star. Errol Flynn? All right, I'll dare you. I'll bet you a nickel it wasn't Errol Flynn, and I dare you to go ask him why he's sitting there with his door open. Go on; he's still there."

The girls looked back and the man seemed not to notice them, his head still in his hands.

"Mama says it's not right to dare anyone and that betting is just plain wrong. It's what turns men into bums."

"We're not going to be bums because I bet you a nickel,

Betty. You'll lose it, but you have more than me. You get more allowance because you're older."

"All right, I'll do it. But not for a dare or a bet. I'll do it because I know I'm right."

And Elizabeth took off back up the street, her little sister skating hard to keep up.

"Mister," Elizabeth said as she neared him. "Oh, Mister," and she slowed down and stopped right in front of him, and he lifted his eyes and both girls gasped.

"It's him," Carolyn said weakly behind her sister.

"Excuse me, sir," said Elizabeth, "but my sister and I were wondering why you're sitting here; I know it's none of our business and please forgive us but we were just curious." Elizabeth said it in one breath and couldn't believe she had just said it. All the time she had been looking at his eyes: the most handsome face in all the world and the saddest eyes she had ever seen. The man put his cigarette out on the curb and didn't say anything.

"I'm sorry to have bothered you," she said. "Let's go, Carolyn." And she turned to skate fast down the street.

"No, wait," the man said. It was the lovely, half-English voice of Flynn, she swore it was. Elizabeth turned. "I'll tell you," he said. "You see, I'm supposed to go to a movie premier tonight. And people will be cheering me and I'll smile and wave. It's all very easy. But there's more than that." He paused. His words were slow and he fumbled in the inside pocket of his tuxedo for a cigarette, but he didn't light it. He held it and looked straight at the girl.

"What would you do," he said, "if you loved life and a doctor told you that, even though you were young, you had less than twenty years to live, if you were lucky? And I'm lucky," he added.

"I'd fire the doctor."

The man looked serious. "Can't do that. Afraid he's one of the best."

Elizabeth thought about it. Twenty years seemed like a long time to her. "I'd probably want to go have a good time, sir."

"That's precisely what I was thinking," and the man slapped his knee. "Never let the world get you down."

"No, sir."

"Never let the world tell you what you can or cannot do."

"Never."

"Travel as much as you can."

"All right."

Then he lapsed into silence again. He gazed at the bit of grass under his shining shoes until Elizabeth thought he had forgotten she was there. She thought she should go. She nodded to Carolyn.

Then she remembered something that Mama had said to Daddy when he was low: "They may not know who you are, Jim, but you know. Now Betty has something for you." And Elizabeth had given him a picture she had drawn of their house when he had been a very important man. Now she wanted to give something to the man in the car, to remind him of who he was. He was a mighty sea captain. She took off her knapsack and rested it at her feet.

"We were at the beach today, sir."

"You were? Well, good for you," the man said enthusiastically. It was the kind of voice Captain Blood used when he wanted to encourage his men.

"Yes, we were, and I picked up a shell, there. This is my sister" — she would not give her name, as the stranger had not given his — "and we keep a shell collection."

The man saluted Carolyn.

"And I would like you to have this shell, sir. You know you can hear the sea roar when you hold it to your ear," Elizabeth said, and she reached into the knapsack, chose the largest shell and handed it to the man.

He looked at the shell on the girl's palm and back at her and didn't take the shell.

"Take it, sir," she said. "It's for you."

"I like the sea," he said. "I always feel at home when I'm on the sea."

"Then you can listen to it now, sir, and you can feel better."

"I feel fine," he said, "but thank you," and he took the seashell and held it to his ear. He was staring down at the little strip of lawn. He was concentrating, Elizabeth knew. He was listening.

And he was still listening when Carolyn went on and Elizabeth stopped at the corner and looked back. She truly hoped he would feel better. She briefly wondered what it would be like to know you were going to die.

Then she streaked down the sidewalk toward her sister. There were long pink bars in the sky to the west, what she had once called the "fingers of God." Mama had liked it when she said that. Now when they walked in the door they would smell whatever Mama was cooking for dinner. Daddy would be reading the paper in his big chair. He would ask them, how was your trip to the beach, and she would tell him about meeting the great swashbuckler, and he would believe her. Elizabeth knew that death was real, but it did not seem possible, not at all, that anyone she knew would ever die. Then she saw the fingers of God touch the mountains to the east, and she knew what she had just thought was true.

Historical Note: Errol Flynn died of a heart attack in 1959, at the age of fifty. He had an "athletic heart," a misleading term for an oversized heart, that causes fainting spells when engaged in vigorous activity and can be the cause of heart attacks in young athletes or in middle-aged people of moderate activity. Flynn fainted on the set during the shooting of boxing or fencing scenes, in *Gentleman Jim* and *The Adventures of Robin Hood*, reporting that he was just tired. (He also had had two near fatal bouts with malaria.) When he volunteered for service in World War II, because of this heart condition he was given a 4F status, which caused him much bitterness and embarrassment. Later, the director of *The Adventures of Don Juan* said that he thought Flynn knew he wasn't going to live long and had decided simply to enjoy himself.

The Vicar and the Witch

Ballycastle, Ireland, 1650

She came from the south. She had a cart, pulled by an ox, two goats and a cow tied to the back of the cart, roots and bulbs and plants piled in the cart, along with a dresser, the wooden frame of a bed, a large trunk, and a fair-haired boy, of about ten, sitting comfortably among it all. The vicar had seen her that day. But he had not seen her face. He saw dark red hair pouring out from the hood of her long green cape. He noticed how she held the reins with one hand, the other stuck in her cape. The villagers soon reported to him that she had only one hand. She told Mrs. Thunder that a cart had run over her right hand when she was a little girl, and they had to cut it off. Mrs. Thunder didn't believe her.

It was about that time the rumors started that the new arrival in Ballycastle was a witch. That and the fact that Dolan had spread it around that she had healed his back, and everyone had seen him roll off the church roof when he was mending the leak and land with a thud on the paving stones, and he had been no good ever since.

She had been in Ballycastle three months now, and the vicar had been watching her every chance he got. He wanted to sec if there were any abnormalities about her besides the hand. It was his responsibility. But he never saw any abnormalities. She intrigued him beyond belief. And he was suspicious of being so intrigued.

He would have his supper late, for from the window of his study, with the curtain mostly drawn, he watched her every evening when she came down the hill to the village well to draw her water. It was his duty. He would wait for the green-hooded figure to appear. He felt excited when he first noticed her dim figure every evening, when he first heard the click of her shoes on the cobbles. Now it was spring, and the days were getting longer, and he could see her figure more clearly. He liked how she walked purposely across the town square to the well and placed her stick with a pail at each end on the cobbles without dropping it noisily, as others did. He admired how she drew the water and filled her pails effortlessly, even gracefully, even with only one hand. Yet he was suspicious of such grace. He noticed she came to the well when everyone else was in having their supper.

He had to talk with her. It was time, and it was his duty, as vicar. He had watched her long enough, and it was inconclusive. Now he had to act. Yet he was afraid to talk to her. No one he knew had actually had a conversation with her. He had faced the enemy in battle. He could force himself to leave his study. He must do so now, while she was still drawing her water. Before he could think anymore he was out his door and across the square.

"Fine spring evening," he said.

If she was shocked by someone suddenly speaking to her, she didn't show it. She looked at him, without saying anything. He was taken aback by the depth of her eyes. He was afraid again. He thought he had seen her before, but he didn't know where. He looked at her slender back as she leaned over the well. Her hood had fallen down.

"What is it you want, vicar?" she said to the well.

He forced himself to come right to the point. The villagers

deserved it. "The people say that you're a witch," the vicar said.

"Let them think what they like," the woman said to the sloshing bucket of water.

"I myself prefer not to think that," he said softly. He wanted to see her face, closely, again, but she still was turned away.

"That is your choice," she said.

"I hear you're an educated woman."

"I can read and write." She was talking now from behind swings of her long red hair, as if she didn't care whether he were there or not. She put her hood up.

"Have you read the English translation of the Bible? Put together by King James?"

"Now I wouldn't read anything by English heretics, would I?"

She had the two pails of water, now, balancing at the end of each shoulder.

"Here, let me help you with that."

She stepped aside, inadvertently swinging one of the pails close to the vicar's head. She laughed, slightly.

"Got to watch yourself, vicar."

"A little water on my boot won't hurt me."

"That's not what I mean." He had seen her smile, then, when she laughed. He saw it through the curtain of her hair as she dipped her head for a moment.

They were walking uphill, now, towards her cottage. He no longer felt any fear, just excitement, as when he saw her dim green-clad figure approach down the hill each evening. Now he was walking up that hill, with her.

"You're consorting with a witch," she said. "You'll lose your flock. You Protestants have a small enough congregation as it is."

"The Scottish settlers are loyal enough. And the new English families. They would know I'm trying to save a soul."

"No Irish soul needs saving. Especially from an Englishman." He saw the edge of a smile again, from behind wisps of hair.

"Where did you come from?" he asked. He was out of breath from walking up the steep hill. It still hurt him when he had to take sudden deep breaths. Once stabbed with a cavalry sword, it never really leaves you, he thought. The woman, who everyone thought was a witch, was unfazed by the walk.

He tried not to look at it. He had done very well by not looking at it the whole time. Of course he had seen it from a distance. But now he was close, and her right wrist, devoid of a hand, was looped over the stick close to him, and he wouldn't look at it. She turned to him now, and he finally looked into her face again.

It was a beautiful face, he thought, with a fine complexion, something you don't see around here that much, and it did seem somehow familiar. It was a flawless complexion, but he was suspicious of such beauty. He wondered if the cures and healings she was purported to give out to gullible villagers actually worked, and if she had used them on herself. She finally stopped on a rise above the village. Her cottage was still a half-mile away. He could see its smoke rising through the trees.

"You know I'm from the south," she said. "And west, if you must know more. And yes, my cures do work. And you may look at my hand, or rather my wrist without a hand. I know you've been straining. And that's not right for you. You shouldn't strain. Are you rested now? And are you following me all the way to my cottage?"

The vicar didn't know what to say. He actually just wanted to keep looking at her face. She had glanced at him as she spoke. He said, "How is your boy?"

"He is fine, thank you. He does the work of a man, now. He'll be finished chopping the wood by the time we get there."

"Why don't you just use the stream up there for your water? Why come all the way down to the village?"

"I want the people to look out their windows and see me once a day. Like you. So they know I don't have wings or claws or horns. I get water like everyone else. I'm no hermit. My son brings vegetables we grow into market. Everyone sees him then." She was looking straight ahead, towards the cottage as she walked.

"They are wonderful vegetables," the vicar said. "I've never seen such vegetables." They were approaching her cottage now, and he wanted to prolong the walk. He wanted to think of things to say. He wanted to see her face again. And he hadn't got the information that he was supposed to get.

"They're the best in the county," she said. He could see her door now. She had a nice, tidy garden in front, with daffodils growing by a little fence.

"This place looks better than when last I saw it. When Collins owned it."

"He left it in a disgraceful state. The lad and I have had lots of work to do. Do you want some tea, then, vicar, or would that send you to hell?" She turned to him and he saw her face, dimly, inside the cave of her hood. Her eyes seemed bright in that dimness, and her face seemed deeply beautiful.

"It's a serious offence, witchcraft," he said suddenly, "and it's more serious in the eyes of God."

"I think we can leave the eyes of God to God," she said. A veil was cast over the brightness of her eyes, then. "It's man I worry about," she said.

"You do confess to witchcraft, then?"

"Is that why you came all this way? To sneak a confession out of me? I stay out of people's way, and they stay out of mine. They like my vegetables and some, more than you think, like my cures and healings. Now is that enough? These pails are getting heavy."

Just then the fair-haired lad opened the door and walked briskly down the path to the gate in the little fence. There, without speaking, she lowered the pails to him. He looked silently at the vicar as he took the stick from his mother's shoulders.

The vicar glanced from son to mother and felt, then, that what he perceived to be his duty didn't matter at all. That hadn't been himself saying those words. He felt ashamed. Just when he was talking to her, finally talking to her, and she had even invited him in for tea, he had destroyed everything by asking her to confess.

If he were honest with himself, he would admit that he really didn't care. He was an enlightened soul. He had been friends with poets, the likes of Robert Herrick, a fellow pastor who preferred poetry to sermons, and he had fought side by side with Richard Lovelace, who had been captured. He himself had written poetry of classical form before the war. He was no Puritan. He was still loyal to the King whose head the Puritans had lopped off last year. The King wouldn't have cared what she did with her peculiar talents, if she had any. He would have liked that she was pretty.

"I'm sorry," he said. "I don't think you're a witch. My parish just wants me to investigate."

"Your parish doesn't care either," she said. "Gives them something to talk about. Something to be afraid of. Something quaint and heathenish and Irish, so they can say, 'See, it's good and well we're ruling these pagan people. We'll bring them God's order'." She laughed. "You're a good sort, vicar; come in and have a mug of tea. You can see my devilish icons, if you like."

The house smelled of baking bread and a mix of herbs hanging from the rafters, most of which the vicar didn't know. The woman spoke something in Gaelic to the boy, who stoked the fire, put a kettle on, and disappeared out the back. Soon the vicar heard the sound of wood chopping again.

The vicar liked the house. He had been in many low Irish cottages since he had arrived a year ago, and they all oppressed him with a sense of darkness and dampness and closeness. This was small like the rest but had light and air. He wasn't sure how she did it. She hung her green cape on a hook by the door, and he watched her scoop the tea from a sack into the pot. She added water from an earthenware jug on the table into the kettle. Her thick hair swung as she moved, another item that added to the rumors of her witchery. Her hair hung loose and seemed like a waterfall that swayed and parted revealing her at times behind it. He would like to stand here a long time and just watch that swaying and the occasional revelation of her face. But he still felt a burning in his chest from the walk. He took short breaths so as not to stir up the pain again.

"I don't have many friends here," she said, looking at him now from behind the waterfall. "In fact, I don't have any. The people I help, they prefer not to recognize me in public. It's nice to have company here."

"Doesn't that bother you? You could mend it."

"Of course it does, but I'm used to it. And that's what I do. I mend. You don't have many friends either, vicar. A foreigner. More foreign than I. A spokesman for a hated religion. Why are you here?"

It was then that the vicar put his hand to his chest and wavered as he stood, and she led him to a chair and sat him down. The pain from the old wound became suddenly unbearable. It happened sometimes, a feeling as though he were being stabbed again, every time he took a breath. The room spun. He heard her son come in the door and she say something in Gaelic again.

The vicar closed his eyes and all he felt was a cool hand, like a lily, on the back of his neck. Then he was aware of her unbuttoning his waistcoat and his shirt. He was about to protest but he couldn't talk. He felt the same coolness and softness now on his chest. Then he felt it grow warm, increasingly, and it felt warm and cooling at the same time, and he could breathe again. He opened his eyes and saw her bent over him. He involuntarily took a sudden deep breath and felt the pain and closed his eyes again. He felt a velvet warmth return, and he reveled in it.

Now he didn't know where he was for awhile and didn't want to know. He felt he was in a glade. There was a clear stream and the sound of its running and some birds, perhaps larks, busy in the trees. It was a scene from one of his pastoral poems from before the war. Then he saw her there, at the edge of the woods. She had long red-gold hair past her waist, a green gown, and had paused, just about to enter the sunlight in the glade. Part of the sunlight had already touched her hair. She said something to him, and he couldn't understand it.

He now knew where he had seen her before. Only her hair had more gold in it, then. Once, as a vision in his old poem, and once again, when he was lying on his back on the ground after the battle at Marston Moor, just when they had started to rip the gold buttons from off his coat and take his boots, for they thought, with the blood on his coat, he was dead, when he was really just lying there in a peace beyond them: the war and what they were fighting for completely forgotten, the pettiness and the horror and the lunacy of man's tragedies having just then swept over him, and his hat, his beautiful plumed Cavalier's hat, of which he had been so proud, he still felt clutched, in a death grip, in his hand. But it wasn't his hand. He was beyond it all. He saw the red-gold haired creature then, standing above the bodies of prone horses and men. She seemed not to mind the chaos of the battlefield. It was all silent there, where she was. He thought she smiled at him. He moved and murmured something, and the ones taking off his boots and buttons yanked off his boots and ran away with them. She knelt beside him. And he didn't die. He became a vicar, instead.

Then his eyes were open and he was looking down at the red cloud of hair. Her left hand was still inside his waistcoat, against his skin, and he could breathe easily again. "I'm sorry," he said.

Her son brought a mug of tea, which the vicar now held in his hands. The aroma was sweet and the steam cleared his head and felt good when he breathed it.

"You were on the losing side, weren't you," she said, "the last of the poet Cavaliers. So you fled here. You're an exile. And now Cromwell's come to Ireland. He's still in the south, you know, getting rid of every last bit of infidel resistance. I was there for awhile, in England, helping with the wounded."

He could not talk. The sunset glow from the window fell on her hair and on her perfect features. She withdrew her hand.

"I was better with my right hand," she said. "I was afraid the power would not come back, but it has now, since I have been in Ballycastle. The power doesn't care which hand. They thought it was the right, for that's the one I used."

"Who?" the vicar managed to say.

"The righteous ones. Cutting off a hand doesn't cut off the power to heal that comes from it, does it? We've managed to fool them haven't we? Both of us," she said.

He looked at her face, at the light touching her smooth skin, and he thought he had not known such beauty existed in the world, before or after the war. He would talk about that beauty in his sermons to his bored congregation, in their foreign land. He would put that beauty in a poem. But he wanted now just to touch that cheek.

A Note on the Type

The body text in this issue is set in Sabon, an old-style typeface by Jan Tschichold (1902 – 1974) based on type by Claude Garamond (1510 ? – 1561). It was released by Linotype, Monotype, and Stempel in 1967.

Longship Press

Longship Press is an independent, small-press publisher of literature, memoir, educational materials, and art. *Nostos*, the literary journal published by Longship Press, seeks poetry, short fiction, and art throughout the year for its two editions each year. Concepts for book publication may be submitted at any time. Please contact the Editor at

info@longshippress.com